PRAYI...
ENGLISH ...

PRAYING WITH

The English Hymn Writers

Compiled and introduced by
TIMOTHY DUDLEY-SMITH

TRI△NGLE

First published 1989
Triangle
SPCK
Holy Trinity Church
Marylebone Road
London NW1 4DU

British Library Cataloguing in Publication Data
Praying with English hymn writers.
1. Christian church. Public worship. Hymns.
Words
I. Dudley-Smith, Timothy
264'.2

ISBN 0-281-04433-3

Typeset by Rowland Phototypesetting Ltd
Bury St Edmunds, Suffolk
Printed in Great Britain by
BPCC Hazell Books Ltd
Aylesbury, Bucks.

Contents

Introduction

Lord David Cecil, giving the Presidential Address to the English Association in 1973, said of the poet Walter de la Mare:

> We each, I think, have authors who speak to us, as it were, on a private line, whose vision of reality has for us a particular and intimate significance: and to whom, therefore, we owe a particular debt. For me de la Mare is one of these few authors.

Many Christians brought up in a tradition of public worship which includes hymn singing will be able to find there a spiritual parallel to this experience. Though C. S. Lewis, for example, disliked what he called 'the church's gang-songs' and declared that 'hymns were (and are) extremely disagreeable to me', yet the present popularity of hymns and hymn singing proves him the exception. Most of us have favourite hymns that 'speak to us' with that special significance which Lord David Cecil identified; and while the tune often plays a considerable part in this, yet it is in the end the text that matters. Perhaps it is no accident that Walter de la Mare, when asked one day in conversation across the tea table from whom he would like to be descended if he could choose his ancestors, named John Wesley and 'the author of "When I survey the wondrous cross"'. For no names stand higher than Isaac Watts and the Wesleys – notably Charles – among the fathers of English hymnody. I take 'English hymnody' to mean hymns written in English; so that by 'the English hymn writers' in the title of this collection, I am referring to authors of hymns in English, and have felt free to include writers without regard to nationality if their work, whether in origin or by translation, comes to us today in English.

The use of the hymn book in private devotion has a well-established history. Part at least of my purpose in preparing this present collection is to help recapture that tradition for a new generation. With this in mind, certain immediate objections must be faced.

First, there is the question of music. Are not most favourite hymns chosen as much, if not more, because of the tune rather than the text? Many congregations would be entirely at home in singing Nathaniel Micklem's vesper hymn:

> Lord, keep us safe this night
> Beneath the stars and moon;
> Pay thou no heed to what we say,
> We only like the tune.

But in this book there are no tunes, except those carried in the reader's head; and this is not all loss, since it affords an opportunity to attend in a new way to the meaning of the words. With some hymns, such concentration proves more than a text can bear; and the words stand revealed as an inadequate and threadbare jingle, serving only as a vehicle for a memorable tune. More often, I believe, the text considered for itself alone will suggest depths and meanings and 'visions of reality' which easily escape us when our congregational worship is borne aloft on wings of song.

Secondly, what is offered in the following pages is often less – sometimes very much less – than a complete hymn. It would be perversely possible to regard it only as a mutilated hymn; and this I would regret. What is set before the reader in these pages should be seen not primarily as a hymn, but as a prayer. By sometimes concentrating on one element in a longer hymn, I hope to focus the attention of the soul in a sharper and less discursive way than would usually be possible if an entire hymn were presented on the page. Sometimes, of course, a text does appear in full. There are plenty of good short hymns; as well as longer hymns so complete in themselves, whether in structure or spirituality or poetry, that to isolate one or two verses would be to do less than justice to the whole. I hope that readers will approach my selections, like Sherlock Holmes with his famous lens, to discover thoughts whose significance may have escaped them on a larger canvas; and will have in mind that what I am inviting them to use devotionally is not so much part of a hymn as a prayer derived from one. If this habit of attending to the text can be acquired in private devotion, it will pay great dividends in public worship. Many of the best treasures of our hymn books lie, so to say, just beneath the surface, and require closer attention than the singer can always offer them.

Thirdly, it may well be asked whether a hymn, essentially a vehicle for corporate worship and devotion, is suitable for individual and private use. I believe this is usually a false distinction. Bernard Manning in his *Essays in Orthodox Dissent* asked the question, 'When did the men of the eighteenth and nineteenth centuries have most fellowship with one another?' and answered it himself: 'At those times when they sang the most individual hymns'. He instances a number to be found in the pages of this book:

> Jesu, Lover of *my* soul
>
> Rock of Ages, cleft for *me*
>
> When *I* survey the wondrous cross

and adds, 'At such moments they had most communion with one another and most impact on the world.' In general, the hymn that best serves the worship of a congregation will have no difficulty in communicating its spiritual power to an individual engaged in private prayer. It was a true instinct that prompted Lord Tonypandy, when asked on the BBC programme 'Desert Island Discs' what book he would most like on a desert island already thoughtfully provided with the Bible and the works of Shakespeare, to choose the Methodist Hymn Book.

There are in this collection certain items which will be unfamiliar to most readers; but they are not the primary purpose of the book. Rather it is hoped that by using this presentation, which devotes each page to a single prayer, readers will find themselves able to approach familiar texts – even texts that have become hackneyed to them by over-familiarity – with new eyes. Let this book be like the Claude mirror, which enables an artist to view the landscape he is painting in a darkened reflection and so be given a wholly new perception of it. It is not unlike the trick which children soon discover, that there is a strange freshness about a familiar scene viewed upside down between your legs!

In the process of making this selection, certain principles have applied. There does not seem, for example, to be a wealth of undiscovered material in the various 'Collected Works' of hymn writers of the past. I have only been able to comb through some of these; and one or two items are included in consequence. But in general, time and the editorial process seem to have winnowed reliably in this field, and the best is already in our hymnals. Any reader of hymns will soon discover, also, that by no means all are prayers; many are hortatory, some declaratory, didactic, narrative or meditative. Indeed, it is instructive to note to whom the words of a hymn are primarily addressed. Some, following Augustine's classic definition, are addressed to God; but others to the singer himself ('Praise, my soul, the King of heaven'), to any believer ('Christian, seek not yet repose'), or to the Church ('Come, let us join our cheerful songs'); and one Christmas hymn contains verses addressed not only to the town of Bethlehem, but to the morning stars also.

Although the items that follow are all in the form of prayers, not all are prayers of intercession. Hymns seem to be better at providing words to describe, or to convey, the movement of the heart towards God; and less successful when they attempt to follow more closely the range and pattern of liturgical intercessions. Almost every item is either drawn from a collection of hymns, or from a section of hymns within a more general book of collected verse. An exception is the Epilogue, 'Vespers', which is indeed by an established hymn writer, but not so far as I know intended to be sung. With the further exception of one or two short items by Charles Wesley, for whom the distinction between hymns and poetry is notoriously blurred, all the rest were written as hymns or have found their way into published hymnals.

This selection is not intended to be in any way representative of authors or periods; it certainly lays no claim to offer the cream of English hymnody. Many hymns of prayer have been omitted which I would have been glad to include. As a reminder that hymn writing is very much a living art, I have found room for one extract each from a number of living authors – and could easily have included more, had space allowed. The text I have sought to follow is generally the 'received text' – that is, the text as it now most commonly appears in mainstream hymnals, unaffected by current doctrinaire principles of revision. This is by no means of course always the text as the author wrote it; but refined by use, by editorial skill, and by the mind of the Church. This means that many a hymn, even when it appears to be given in full, is considerably shorter than the author's original. It may also imply certain changes to which we have become so accustomed that to us they are now part of what I have called the 'received text'. To take one well-known example, the hymn 'Abide with me' as Henry Lyte wrote it consists of eight verses, including one which begins 'Not a brief glance I beg . . .' and another 'Come not in terrors . . .'. But even in the three verses quoted in this book there are two or three significant changes from the original. We sing, for example 'The darkness deepens' rather than 'The darkness thickens' in the first verse; and 'Shine through the gloom' is now the invariable improvement on the author's 'Speak through the gloom'. This book therefore follows what I consider the generally received text, even where that may differ from the author's original.

The arrangement I have adopted is based on six chapters, as set out in the table of contents. The subheadings under each are not an exhaustive list, but merely suggestive of the kind of entries to be found in each section. Inevitably there will be an element of the arbitrary about any pattern of selection, and because in some instances a given extract could as properly be included under some other heading, I have added at the end of the book an 'Index of First Lines' to help in locating prayers where the opening words are known, either of the whole hymn, or of any extract used in this book. I hope similarly that the 'Index of Sources' may be of use to a reader who wants to track down the full version or a hymn represented here by only a verse or two; while the 'Index of Hymn Writers' will serve to give an indication of period and of the most basic information about each author. There are two special categories of prayer which I have grouped together; those concerning Holy Communion, which will be found at the end of Chapter 1; and those connected with the reading of Scripture, which come at the end of Chapter 3. The Prologue (from which I have borrowed my chapter headings) will be familiar to almost all who sing hymns; the Epilogue much less so. I discovered it in John Baillie's *A Diary of Readings* and have often returned to it. It speaks to me, in Lord David Cecil's phrase, 'on a private line', which is why I have stretched the rules to include it here.

Even so small a book as this must gratefully acknowledge much help received from others. I thank Myrtle Powley of SPCK for inviting me to contribute to this series, Joyce Horn of the Oxford University Press, Raymond Glover of the Church Hymnal Corporation,

New York, Mary Louise VanDyke of the Dictionary of American Hymnology, and Brenda Lewis of the Evangelical Movement of Wales for help with biographical information; and the Reverend Susan M. Nuttall for an account of her great-aunt, Lucy A. Bennett.

Writing on dramatic poetry, T. S. Eliot said once that 'in intense emotions, and in its approach to the permanent and the universal, the human soul tends to express itself in verse.' I hope that, for some reader, this little book may contribute to that experience.

Timothy Dudley-Smith
Ruan Minor, 1989

'A verse may find him, who a sermon flies,
And turn delight into a sacrifice.'

George Herbert,
from 'The Church-porch'

PROLOGUE

A heart renewed
from Psalm 51

O for a heart to praise my God,
   A heart from sin set free,
A heart that always feels thy blood
   So freely spilt for me;

A heart resigned, submissive, meek,
   My great Redeemer's throne,
Where only Christ is heard to speak,
   Where Jesus reigns alone;

A humble, lowly, contrite heart,
   Believing, true, and clean;
Which neither life nor death can part
   From him that dwells within;

A heart in every thought renewed,
   And full of love divine;
Perfect, and right, and pure, and good,
   A copy, Lord, of thine!

Thy nature, gracious Lord, impart;
   Come quickly from above,
Write thy new name upon my heart,
   Thy new, best name of love.

Charles Wesley

1. TO PRAISE MY GOD
The approach to worship

Love and grace – The gift of praise
The universal song – Earth and heaven
The new creation – Thankfulness
The school of prayer
Holy Communion

How good is the God we adore,
Our faithful, unchangeable Friend!
His love is as great as his power,
And knows neither measure nor end!

'Tis Jesus, the first and the last,
Whose Spirit shall guide us safe home;
We'll praise him for all that is past,
We'll trust him for all that's to come.

Joseph Hart

The fire of the Spirit

Come down, O Love divine,
Seek thou this soul of mine,
And visit it with thine own ardour glowing;
O Comforter, draw near,
Within my heart appear,
And kindle it, thy holy flame bestowing.

O let it freely burn,
Till earthly passions turn
To dust and ashes, in its heat consuming;
And let thy glorious light
Shine ever on my sight,
And clothe me round, the while my path illuming.

Let holy charity
Mine outward vesture be,
And lowliness become mine inner clothing;
True lowliness of heart,
Which takes the humbler part,
And o'er its own shortcomings weeps with
    loathing.

And so the yearning strong,
With which the soul will long,
Shall far outpass the power of human telling;
For none can guess its grace,
Till he become the place
Wherein the Holy Spirit makes his dwelling.

Bianco da Siena
translated by Richard Frederick Littledale

A flame of love

Spirit of God, descend upon my heart;
    Wean it from earth; through all its pulses move;
Stoop to my weakness, mighty as thou art,
    And make me love thee as I ought to love.

Hast thou not bid me love thee, God and King –
    All, all thine own, soul, heart, and strength, and
      mind?
I see thy cross – there teach my heart to cling:
    O let me seek thee, and O let me find!   .

Teach me to feel that thou art always nigh;
    Teach me the struggles of the soul to bear,
To check the rising doubt, the rebel sigh;
    Teach me the patience of unanswered prayer.

Teach me to love thee as thine angels love,
    One holy passion filling all my frame –
The baptism of the heaven-descended Dove,
    My heart an altar, and thy love the flame.

George Croly

Unmeasurable grace

Come, dearest Lord, descend and dwell
   By faith and love in every breast;
Then shall we know and taste and feel
   The joys that cannot be expressed.

Come, fill our hearts with inward strength,
   Make our enlargèd souls possess
And learn the height and breadth and length
   Of thine unmeasurable grace.

Isaac Watts

Sovereign mercy

'Tis not that I did choose thee,
   For, Lord, that could not be;
This heart would still refuse thee
   Hadst thou not chosen me.
Thou from the sin that stained me
   Hast cleansed and set me free;
Of old thou hast ordained me,
   That I should live to thee.

'Twas sovereign mercy called me,
   And taught my opening mind;
The world had else enthralled me,
   To heavenly glories blind.
My heart owns none above thee;
   For thy rich grace I thirst;
This knowing, if I love thee,
   Thou must have loved me first.

Josiah Conder

The gift of praise

Fill thou my life, O Lord my God,
    In every part with praise,
That my whole being may proclaim
    Thy being and thy ways.

Not for the lip of praise alone
    Nor e'en the praising heart
I ask, but for a life made up
    Of praise in every part.

So shall no part of day or night
    From sacredness be free;
But all my life, in every step,
    Be fellowship with thee.

Horatius Bonar

The universal song

From all that dwell below the skies
Let the Creator's praise arise:
Let the Redeemer's name be sung,
Through every land, by every tongue:

Eternal are thy mercies, Lord;
Eternal truth attends thy word:
Thy praise shall sound from shore to shore,
Till suns shall rise and set no more.

Isaac Watts

Earth and heaven

My God, I thank thee, who hast made
   The earth so bright,
So full of splendour and of joy,
   Beauty and light;
So many glorious things are here,
   Noble and right.

I thank thee too that all our joy
   Is touched with pain,
That shadows fall on brightest hours,
   That thorns remain,
So that earth's bliss may be our guide,
   And not our chain.

I thank thee, Lord, that here our souls,
   Though amply blest,
Can never find, although they seek,
   A perfect rest,
Nor ever shall, until they lean
   On Jesu's breast.

Adelaide Anne Proctor

The new creation

I praised the earth, in beauty seen
With garlands gay of various green;
I praised the sea, whose ample field
Shone glorious as a silver shield;
And earth and ocean seemed to say
'Our beauties are but for a day!'

I praised the sun, whose chariot rolled
On wheels of amber and of gold;
I praised the moon, whose softer eye
Gleamed sweetly through the summer sky!
And moon and sun in answer said,
'Our days of light are numberèd!'

O God! O Good beyond compare!
If thus thy meaner works are fair,
If thus thy bounties gild the span
Of ruined earth and sinful man,
How glorious must the mansion be
Where thy redeemed shall dwell with thee!

Reginald Heber

Thankfulness

Now thank we all our God,
   With hearts and hands and voices,
Who wondrous things has done,
   In whom his world rejoices;
Who from our mothers' arms
   Has blessed us on our way
With countless gifts of love,
   And still is ours today.

O may this bounteous God
   Through all our life be near us,
With ever joyful hearts
   And blessèd peace to cheer us;
And keep us in his grace,
   And guide us when perplexed,
And free us from all ills
   In this world and the next.

Martin Rinkart
translated by Catherine Winkworth

The school of prayer

Prayer is the soul's sincere desire,
Uttered or unexpressed;
The motion of a hidden fire,
That trembles in the breast.

Prayer is the Christian's vital breath,
The Christian's native air,
His watchword at the gates of death:
He enters heaven with prayer.

O thou by whom we come to God,
The Life, the Truth, the Way,
The path of prayer thyself hast trod:
Lord, teach us how to pray.

James Montgomery

To pray aright

Lord, teach us how to pray aright,
 With reverence and with fear;
Though dust and ashes in thy sight,
 We may, we must draw near.

We perish if we cease from prayer;
 O grant us power to pray!
And, when to meet thee we prepare,
 Lord, meet us by the way.

James Montgomery

Before Holy Communion: a recollection

Thy body, broken for my sake,
My bread from heaven shall be;
Thy cup of blessing I will take,
And thus remember thee.

Can I Gethsemane forget?
Or there thy conflict see,
Thine agony and bloody sweat,
And not remember thee?

When to the cross I turn mine eyes,
And rest on Calvary,
O Lamb of God, my sacrifice,
I must remember thee:

Remember thee, and all thy pains,
And all thy love to me;
Yea, while a breath, a pulse remains,
Will I remember thee.

James Montgomery

Before Holy Communion:
an act of faith

Here, O my Lord, I see thee face to face;
    Here would I touch and handle things unseen,
Here grasp with firmer hand the eternal grace,
    And all my weariness upon thee lean.

Here would I feed upon the bread of God,
    Here drink with thee the royal wine of heaven;
Here would I lay aside each earthly load,
    Here taste afresh the calm of sin forgiven.

Mine is the sin, but thine the righteousness;
    Mine is the guilt, but thine the cleansing blood;
Here is my robe, my refuge, and my peace –
    Thy blood, thy righteousness, O Lord, my God.

Horatius Bonar

Before Holy Communion:
trusting in Christ

Great and glorious Father, humbly we adore thee,
   Poor and weak and helpless sinners in thine
      eyes;
Yet, in meek obedience, low we fall before thee,
   Trusting, pleading only Jesus' sacrifice.

Bowed beneath thy footstool, yet with boldness
      pleading
   This the only plea on which our hope relies,
Unto thee, O Father, all thy mercy needing,
   Make we this memorial of Christ's sacrifice.

Hath he died to save us, in his love so tender,
   And shall we repay him nought but fruitless
      sighs?
Nay, our souls and bodies, all we have we render:
   Father, for his sake accept our sacrifice.

William Walsham How

Before Holy Communion: abiding in Christ

Be known to us in breaking bread,
  But do not then depart;
Saviour, abide with us, and spread
  Thy table in our heart.

There sup with us in love divine;
  Thy body and thy blood,
That living bread, that heavenly wine,
  Be our immortal food.

James Montgomery

Before Holy Communion: united to Christ

Come, risen Lord, and deign to be our guest;
   Nay, let us be thy guests; the feast is thine;
Thyself at thine own board make manifest,
   In thine own sacrament of bread and wine.

One with each other, Lord, for one in thee,
   Who art one Saviour and one living Head;
Then open thou our eyes, that we may see;
   Be known to us in breaking of the bread.

George Wallace Briggs

At Holy Communion:
the cross of Christ

And now, O Father, mindful of the love
    That bought us, once for all, on Calvary's tree,
And having with us him that pleads above,
    We here present, we here spread forth to thee
That only offering perfect in thine eyes,
The one true, pure, immortal sacrifice.

Look, Father, look on his anointed face,
    And only look on us as found in him;
Look not on our misusings of thy grace,
    Our prayer so languid, and our faith so dim:
For lo! Between our sins and their reward
We set the passion of thy Son our Lord.

William Bright

At Holy Communion:
the life of heaven

Saviour, I seek your face,
   I here confess you;
Within your holy place
   I kneel to bless you.
I gaze upon your board –
   Love's mystic token;
For me, your blood outpoured,
   Your body broken:
     I fall, amazed, before you;
     I worship, I adore you.

Saviour, I seek your face
   In sweet communion;
Here let me taste your grace
   In holy union;
Here let me find rebirth
   In sins forgiven;
Here let me know on earth
   The life of heaven:
     I fall, amazed, before you;
     I worship, I adore you.

Margaret Clarkson

After Holy Communion: walking in the light

Strengthen for service, Lord, the hands
   That holy things have taken;
Let ears that now have heard thy songs
   To clamour never waken.

Lord, may the tongues which 'Holy' sang
   Keep free from all deceiving;
The eyes which saw thy love be bright,
   Thy blessèd hope perceiving.

The feet that tread thy hallowed courts
   From light do thou not banish;
The bodies by thy body fed
   With thy new life replenish.

from the Syriac Liturgy of Malabar
translated by
Charles William Humphreys and Percy Dearmer

2. FROM SIN SET FREE
Penitence and pardon

Man of sorrows – The sinner's friend
The cross – The saving Name
Mercy – Repentance – Saviour and Lord
The look of faith
Coming to Christ – No condemnation
Grace and pardon – Peace and wholeness
Grieve not the Spirit

Lord Jesus, think on me,
And purge away my sin;
From earthborn passions set me free,
And make me pure within.

Lord Jesus, think on me
With care and woe oppressed;
Let me thy loving servant be,
And taste thy promised rest.

Synesius of Cyrene
translated by
Allen William Chatfield

Man of sorrows

O sacred head, sore wounded,
  Defiled and put to scorn;
O kingly head, surrounded
  With mocking crown of thorn:
What sorrow mars thy grandeur?
  Can death thy bloom deflower?
O countenance whose splendour
  The hosts of heaven adore.

I pray thee, Jesus, own me,
  Me, Shepherd good, for thine;
Who to thy fold hast won me,
  And fed with truth divine.
Me guilty, me refuse not,
  Incline thy face to me,
This comfort that I lose not,
  On earth to comfort thee.

In thy most bitter passion
  My heart to share doth cry,
With thee for my salvation
  Upon the cross to die.
Ah, keep my heart thus movèd
  To stand thy cross beneath,
To mourn thee, well-belovèd,
  Yet thank thee for thy death.

My days are few, O fail not,
  With thine immortal power,
To hold me that I quail not
  In death's most fearful hour:
That I may fight befriended,
  And see in my last strife
To me thine arms extended
  Upon the cross of life.

Paulus Gerhardt
translated by Robert Seymour Bridges

The sinner's friend

When at thy footstool, Lord, I bend,
   And plead with thee for mercy there,
O think thou of the sinner's Friend,
   And for his sake receive my prayer!
O think not of my shame and guilt,
   My thousand stains of deepest dye:
Think of the blood which Jesus spilt,
   And let that blood my pardon buy.

O think upon thy holy word,
   And every plighted promise there –
How prayer should evermore be heard,
   And how thy glory is to spare.
O think not of my doubts and fears,
   My strivings with thy grace divine:
Think upon Jesu's woes and tears,
   And let his merits stand for mine.

Henry Francis Lyte

The cross uplifted

Oh, teach me what it meaneth,
  That cross uplifted high,
With one, the Man of Sorrows,
  Condemned to bleed and die!
Oh, teach me what it cost thee
  To make a sinner whole;
And teach me, Saviour, teach me
  The value of a soul!

Oh, teach me what it meaneth,
  That sacred crimson tide,
The blood and water flowing
  From thine own wounded side.
Teach me that if none other
  Had sinned, but I alone,
Yet still, thy blood, Lord Jesus,
  Thine only, must atone.

Oh, teach me what it meaneth,
  For I am full of sin;
And grace alone can reach me,
  And love alone can win.
Oh, teach me, for I need thee,
  I have no hope beside,
The chief of all the sinners
  For whom the Saviour died!

Lucy Ann Bennett

The saving Name

Approach, my soul, the mercy-seat,
Where Jesus answers prayer;
There humbly fall before his feet,
For none can perish there.

Thy promise is my only plea,
With this I venture nigh:
Thou callest burdened souls to thee,
And such, O Lord, am I.

Bowed down beneath a load of sin,
By Satan sorely pressed,
By war without and fears within,
I come to thee for rest.

Be thou my shield and hiding-place,
That, sheltered near thy side,
I may my fierce accuser face,
And tell him, thou hast died.

O wondrous love, to bleed and die,
To bear the cross and shame,
That guilty sinners, such as I,
Might plead thy gracious name.

John Newton

God be merciful

Goodness I have none to plead,
  Sinfulness in all I see,
I can only bring my need;
  God be merciful to me.

Broken heart and downcast eyes
  Dare not lift themselves to thee;
Yet thou canst interpret sighs:
  God be merciful to me.

John Samuel Bewley Monsell

Vain repentances

Times without number have I prayed,
   This only once forgive, .
Relapsing, when thy hand was stayed
   And suffered me to live:
Yet now the kingdom of thy peace,
   Lord, to my heart restore,
Forgive my vain repentances,
   And bid me sin no more.

Charles Wesley

The double cure

Rock of Ages, cleft for me,
Let me hide myself in thee;
Let the water and the blood,
From thy riven side which flowed,
Be of sin the double cure,
Cleanse me from its guilt and power.

Not the labours of my hands
Can fulfil thy law's demands;
Could my zeal no respite know,
Could my tears for ever flow,
All for sin could not atone:
Thou must save, and thou alone.

Nothing in my hand I bring,
Simply to thy cross I cling;
Naked, come to thee for dress;
Helpless, look to thee for grace;
Foul, I to the fountain fly;
Wash me, Saviour, or I die.

Augustus Montague Toplady

Conquered by Christ

Come, O thou all-victorious Lord,
   Thy power to us make known;
Strike with the hammer of thy word,
   And break these hearts of stone.

Conclude us first in unbelief,
   And freely then release;
Fill every soul with sacred grief,
   And then with sacred peace.

Our desperate state through sin declare,
   And speak our sins forgiven;
By perfect holiness prepare,
   And take us up to heaven.

Charles Wesley

Hear and save

Lord of all, to whom alone
All our hearts' desires are known,
When we stand before thy throne,
     Jesu, hear and save.

Saviour, who didst not condemn
Those who touched thy garments' hem,
Mercy show to us and them:
     Jesu, hear and save.

Son of Man, before whose eyes
Every secret open lies,
At thy great and last assize,
     Jesu, hear and save.

Cyril Argentine Alington

The look of faith

My faith looks up to thee,
Thou Lamb of Calvary,
   Saviour divine:
Now hear me while I pray;
Take all my guilt away;
O let me from this day
   Be wholly thine!

May thy rich grace impart
Strength to my fainting heart,
   My zeal inspire;
As thou hast died for me,
O may my love to thee
Pure, warm, and changeless be,
   A living fire.

Ray Palmer

Coming to Christ

Just as I am, without one plea
But that thy blood was shed for me,
And that thou bidd'st me come to thee,
O Lamb of God, I come!

Just as I am, though tossed about
With many a conflict, many a doubt,
Fightings and fears within, without,
O Lamb of God, I come!

Just as I am, poor, wretched, blind;
Sight, riches, healing of the mind,
Yea, all I need, in thee to find,
O Lamb of God, I come!

Just as I am, thou wilt receive,
Wilt welcome, pardon, cleanse, relieve;
Because thy promise I believe,
O Lamb of God, I come!

Just as I am – thy love unknown
Has broken every barrier down –
Now to be thine, yea, thine alone,
O Lamb of God, I come!

Just as I am, of that free love
The breadth, length, depth, and height to prove,
Here for a season, then above,
O Lamb of God, I come!

Charlotte Elliott

No condemnation

And can it be that I should gain
   An interest in the Saviour's blood?
Died he for me, who caused his pain?
   For me, who him to death pursued?
Amazing love! How can it be
That thou, my God, shouldst die for me?

No condemnation now I dread;
   Jesus, and all in him, is mine!
Alive in him, my living Head,
   And clothed in righteousness divine,
Bold I approach the eternal throne,
And claim the crown, through Christ, my own.

Charles Wesley

Repentance and restoration

Shapen in frailty, born in sin,
   From error how shall I depart?
Lo, thou requirest truth within;
   Lord, write thy truth upon my heart.

Me through the blood of sprinkling make
   Pure from defilement, white as snow;
Heal me for my Redeemer's sake;
   Then joy and gladness I shall know.

A perfect heart in me create,
   Renew my soul in innocence;
Cast not the suppliant from thy gate,
   Nor take thine Holy Spirit hence.

Thy consolations, as of old,
   Now to my troubled mind restore;
By thy free Spirit's might uphold
   And guide my steps, to fall no more.

James Montgomery

Peace and wholeness

Shine from the cross to me, then all is peace;
Shine from the throne, then all my troubles cease;
Speak but the word, and sadness quits my soul;
Touch but my hand with thine, and I am whole.

Horatius Bonar

Grieve not the Spirit

Where is the blessedness I knew
When first I saw the Lord?
Where is the soul-refreshing view
Of Jesus and his word?

Return, O holy Dove, return,
Sweet messenger of rest;
I hate the sins that made thee mourn,
And drove thee from my breast.

The dearest idol I have known,
Whate'er that idol be,
Help me to tear it from thy throne,
And worship only thee.

So shall my walk be close with God,
Calm and serene my frame;
So purer light shall mark the road
That leads me to the Lamb.

William Cowper

3. IN EVERY THOUGHT RENEWED
Newness of life

Lord, be thy word my rule,
In it may I rejoice;
Thy glory be my aim,
Thy holy will my choice.

Thy promises my hope;
Thy providence my guard;
Thine arm my strong support;
Thyself my great reward.

Christopher Wordsworth

The vision of God

Be thou my vision, O Lord of my heart,
Be all else but naught to me, save that thou art;
   Be thou my best thought in the day and the
      night,
   Both waking and sleeping, thy presence my
      light.

Riches I heed not, nor man's empty praise:
Be thou mine inheritance now and always;
   Be thou and thou only the first in my heart:
   O Sovereign of heaven, my treasure thou art.

High King of heaven, thou heaven's bright Sun,
O grant me its joys after victory is won;
   Great Heart of my own heart, whatever befall,
   Still be thou my vision, O Ruler of all.

From the Irish, c.8th century
translated by Mary Elizabeth Byrne
versified by Eleanor Henrietta Hull

The secret of the Lord

Blest are the pure in heart,
　For they shall see our God:
The secret of the Lord is theirs;
　Their soul is Christ's abode.

Lord, we thy presence seek;
　May ours this blessing be;
Give us a pure and lowly heart,
　A temple meet for thee.

John Keble, verse 1.
Verse 2 is anonymous from *Hall's Psalms and Hymns*, 1836

The new year

Father, let me dedicate
All this year to thee,
In whatever worldly state
Thou wilt have me be:
Not from sorrow, pain or care
Freedom dare I claim;
This alone shall be my prayer:
'Glorify thy name.'

If thou callest to the cross,
And its shadow come,
Turning all my gain to loss,
Shrouding heart and home;
Let me think how thy dear Son
To his glory came,
And in deepest woe pray on:
'Glorify thy name.'

If in mercy thou wilt spare
Joys that yet are mine;
If on life, serene and fair,
Brighter rays may shine;
Let my glad heart, while it sings,
Thee in all proclaim,
And whate'er the future brings,
Glorify thy name.

Lawrence Tuttiett

The new day

Lord, as I wake I turn to you,
  Yourself the first thought of my day;
My King, my God, whose help is sure,
  Yourself the help for which I pray.

Your loving gifts of grace to me,
  Those favours I could never earn,
Call for my thanks in praise and prayer,
  Call me to love you in return.

Lord, make my life a life of love,
  Keep me from sin in all I do;
Lord, make your law my only law,
  Your will my will, for love of you.

Brian Foley

Duty and delight

Teach me, my God and King,
   In all things thee to see,
And what I do in anything,
   To do it as for thee.

A servant with this clause
   Makes drudgery divine;
Who sweeps a room, as for thy laws,
   Makes that and the action fine.

George Herbert

An instrument of peace

O Master Christ, draw near to take
your undisputed place;
my gifts and faculties remake,
form and re-fashion for your sake
an instrument of peace.

O Master Christ, I choose to sow
in place of hatred, love;
where wounds and injuries are now
may healing and forgiveness grow
as gifts from God above.

O Master Christ, I choose to plant
hope where there is despair;
a warmth of joy, a shaft of light
where darkness has diminished sight,
where sorrow leaves its scar.

O Master Christ, make this my goal –
less to receive than give;
to sympathise – and to make whole
to understand and to console
and so, through death, to live.

David Mowbray

Stillness

Dear Lord and Father of mankind,
   Forgive our foolish ways;
Reclothe us in our rightful mind;
In purer lives thy service find,
   In deeper reverence, praise.

Drop thy still dews of quietness,
   Till all our strivings cease;
Take from our souls the strain and stress,
And let our ordered lives confess
   The beauty of thy peace.

John Greenleaf Whittier

Servants of Christ

Lord, speak to me, that I may speak
  In living echoes of thy tone;
As thou hast sought, so let me seek
  Thy erring children lost and lone.

O strengthen me, that, while I stand
  Firm on the rock, and strong in thee,
I may stretch out a loving hand
  To wrestlers with the troubled sea.

O teach me, Lord, that I may teach
  The precious things thou dost impart;
And wing my words, that they may reach
  The hidden depths of many a heart.

Frances Ridley Havergal

One in Christ

Jesus, Lord, we look to thee,
Let us in thy name agree;
Show thyself the Prince of Peace;
Bid our jarring conflicts cease.

Let us for each other care,
Each the other's burden bear,
To thy church the pattern give,
Show how true believers live.

Make us of one heart and mind,
Courteous, pitiful, and kind,
Lowly, meek in thought and word,
Altogether like our Lord.

Charles Wesley

Christic in the home

Lord of the home, your only Son
   Received a mother's tender love,
And from an earthly father won
   His vision of your home above.

Teach us to keep our homes so fair
   That, were our Lord a child once more,
He might be glad our hearth to share,
   And find a welcome at our door.

Albert Frederick Bayly

The light of Scripture

The heavens declare thy glory, Lord,
   In every star thy wisdom shines;
But when our eyes behold thy word,
   We read thy name in fairer lines.

Sun, moon, and stars convey thy praise
   Round this whole earth, and never stand;
So when thy truth began its race,
   It touched and glanced on every land.

Nor shall thy spreading gospel rest
   Till through the world thy truth has run;
Till Christ has all the nations blest,
   That see the light or feel the sun.

Thy noblest wonders here we view,
   In souls renewed, and sins forgiven;
Lord, cleanse my sins, my soul renew,
   And make thy word my guide to heaven.

Isaac Watts

Reading the Bible:
the humble mind

Lord, for ever at thy side
let my place and portion be,
strip me of the robe of pride,
clothe me with humility.

When I come before thy word,
quiet my anxiety;
teach me thou alone art Lord,
let my heart find rest in thee.

James Montgomery and
Charles Philip Price

Reading the Bible:
Christ in the Scriptures

Father of mercies, in thy word
　　What endless glory shines!
For ever be thy name adored
　　For these celestial lines.

O may these heavenly pages be
　　My ever dear delight,
And still new beauties may I see,
　　And still increasing light.

Divine instructor, gracious Lord,
　　Be thou for ever near;
Teach me to love thy sacred word,
　　And view my Saviour here.

Anne Steele

Reading the Bible:
Christian assurance

Lord, give us eyes to see
  The wonders of thy law,
Its justice, truth, and purity;
  That, touched with holy awe,
Conscience, no longer dumb,
  Sin's guilt and curse may own;
Then, from the storm of wrath to come,
  Cling to the cross alone.

Lord, give us hearts to feel
  The bliss of pardoning love,
The Spirit's witness, and the seal
  Of sonship from above;
So shall our lips express,
  So in our actions shine,
The beauty of true holiness,
  The proof that we are thine.

James Montgomery

Reading the Bible:
the listening heart

Master, speak! Thy servant heareth,
    Waiting for thy gracious word,
Longing for thy voice that cheereth;
    Master, let it now be heard.
I am listening, Lord, for thee;
What hast thou to say to me?

Master, speak! Though least and lowest,
    Let me not unheard depart;
Master, speak! For O thou knowest
    All the yearning of my heart,
Knowest all its truest need;
Speak, and make me blest indeed.

Frances Ridley Havergal

Reading the Bible:
seeking God's will

Spirit of truth, thy word reveal,
   Its treasures open wide;
Lead me to see my Father's will,
   And in that will abide.

James Holroyde

Reading the Bible:
feeding on Christ

Break thou the bread of life,
    O Lord, to me,
As thou didst break the loaves
    Beside the sea.
Beyond the sacred page
    I seek thee, Lord;
My spirit longs for thee,
    O living Word!

Mary Artemisia Lathbury

4. WHERE JESUS REIGNS ALONE
Christ in the heart

Wayward souls – Celestial fire
The opened door – My heart your home
Seeking and finding
Unseen but not unknown
Captive to Christ – Christ alone
Treasure in heaven – So rich a crown

And dost thou say, 'Ask what thou wilt'?
Lord, I would seize the golden hour;
I pray to be released from guilt,
And freed from sin and Satan's power.

More of thy presence, Lord, impart,
More of thine image let me bear;
Erect thy throne within my heart,
And reign without a rival there.

John Newton

Wayward souls

Spirit of God, that moved of old
Upon the waters' darkened face,
Come, when our faithless hearts are cold,
And stir them with an inward grace.

Thou that art power and peace combined,
All highest strength, all purest love,
The rushing of the mighty wind,
The brooding of the gentle dove,

Come give us still thy powerful aid,
And urge us on, and keep us thine;
Nor leave the hearts that once were made
Fit temples for thy grace divine;

Nor let us quench thy sevenfold light;
But still with softest breathings stir
Our wayward souls, and lead us right,
O Holy Ghost, the comforter.

Cecil Frances Alexander

Celestial fire

O thou who camest from above
   The pure celestial fire to impart,
Kindle a flame of sacred love
   On the mean altar of my heart!

There let it for thy glory burn
   With inextinguishable blaze,
And trembling to its source return,
   In humble prayer and fervent praise.

Jesus, confirm my heart's desire
   To work, and speak, and think for thee;
Still let me guard the holy fire,
   And still stir up thy gift in me:

Ready for all thy perfect will,
   My acts of faith and love repeat,
Till death thy endless mercies seal,
   And make the sacrifice complete.

Charles Wesley

The opened door

Come in, O come! the door stands open now;
I knew thy voice: Lord Jesus, it was thou;
The sun has set long since; the storms begin;
'Tis time for thee, my Saviour, O come in!

Alas, ill-ordered shows the dreary room;
The household-stuff lies heaped amidst the gloom;
The table empty stands, the couch undressed;
Ah, what a welcome for the eternal guest!

I seek no more to alter things, or mend,
Before the coming of so great a friend;
All were at best unseemly; and 'twere ill
Beyond all else to keep thee waiting still.

Come, not to find, but make this troubled heart
A dwelling worthy of thee as thou art;
To chase the gloom, the terror, and the sin:
Come, all thyself, yea come, Lord Jesus, in!

Handley Carr Glyn Moule

The gift of love

What can I give him,
   Poor as I am?
If I were a shepherd
   I would bring a lamb;
If I were a wise man
   I would do my part;
Yet what I can I give him –
   Give my heart.

Christina Georgina Rossetti

Christ within

Were earth a thousand times as fair,
Beset with gold and jewels rare,
   She yet were far too poor to be
   A narrow cradle, Lord, for thee.

Ah, dearest Jesus, holy child,
Make thee a bed, soft, undefiled,
   Within my heart, that it may be
   A quiet chamber kept for thee.

Martin Luther
translated by Catherine Winkworth

My heart your home

Lord, you need no house,
no manger now, nor tomb;
yet come, I pray, to make
my heart your home.

Lord, you need no gift,
for all things come from you;
receive what you have given –
my heart renew.

Lord, you need no skill
to make your likeness known;
create your image here –
my heart your throne.

Christopher Martin Idle

Seeking and finding

Jesu, thou joy of loving hearts,
  Thou fount of life, thou light of men,
From the best bliss that earth imparts
  We turn unfilled to thee again.

Thy truth unchanged hath ever stood;
  Thou savest those that on thee call;
To them that seek thee thou art good,
  To them that find thee, all in all.

O Jesus, ever with us stay;
  Make all our moments calm and bright;
Chase the dark night of sin away;
  Shed o'er the world thy holy light.

From the Latin, 12th century
translated by Ray Palmer

Unseen but not unknown

Jesus, these eyes have never seen
That radiant form of thine;
The veil of sense hangs dark between
Thy blessed face and mine.

Yet, though I have not seen, and still
Must rest in faith alone,
I love thee, dearest Lord, and will,
Unseen but not unknown.

Ray Palmer

One with God

Breathe on me, Breath of God;
    Fill me with life anew,
That I may love what thou dost love,
    And do what thou wouldst do.

Breathe on me, Breath of God,
    Till I am wholly thine,
Until this earthly part of me
    Glows with thy fire divine.

Breathe on me, Breath of God;
    So shall I never die,
But live with thee the perfect life
    Of thine eternity.

Edwin Hatch

The love of Jesus

Jesu, thy boundless love to me
　No thought can reach, no tongue declare;
O knit my thankful heart to thee,
　And reign without a rival there:
Thine wholly, thine alone, I am;
Be thou alone my constant flame.

Still let thy love point out my way;
　How wondrous things thy love has wrought!
Still lead me, lest I go astray;
　Direct my word, inspire my thought;
And if I fall, soon may I hear
Thy voice, and know that love is near.

Paulus Gerhardt
translated by John Wesley

Christ's bondslave

Make me a captive, Lord,
    And then I shall be free;
Force me to render up my sword,
    And I shall conqueror be.
I sink in life's alarms
    When by myself I stand;
Imprison me within thine arms,
    And strong shall be my hand.

George Matheson

Christ alone

If a sinner such as I
  May to thy great glory live,
All my actions sanctify,
  All my words and thoughts receive;
Claim me for thy service, claim
All I have and all I am.

Take my soul and body's powers;
  Take my memory, mind, and will,
All my goods, and all my hours,
  All I know, and all I feel,
All I think, or speak, or do;
Take my heart, but make it new.

Now, O God, thine own I am,
  Now I give thee back thine own;
Freedom, friends, and health, and fame
  Consecrate to thee alone:
Thine I live, thrice happy I;
Happier still if thine I die.

Charles Wesley

Treasure in heaven

Take my life, and let it be
Consecrated, Lord, to thee;
Take my moments and my days,
Let them flow in ceaseless praise.

Take my will, and make it thine;
It shall be no longer mine;
Take my heart – it is thine own;
It shall be thy royal throne.

Take my love; my Lord, I pour
At thy feet its treasure-store;
Take myself, and I will be
Ever, only, all for thee.

Frances Ridley Havergal

To live for Christ

O dearest Lord, thy sacred head
  With thorns was pierced for me;
O pour thy blessing on my head,
  That I may think for thee.

O dearest Lord, thy sacred hands
  With nails were pierced for me;
O shed thy blessing on my hands,
  That they may work for thee.

O dearest Lord, thy sacred feet
  With nails were pierced for me;
O pour thy blessing on my feet,
  That they may follow thee.

O dearest Lord, thy sacred heart
  With spear was pierced for me;
O pour thy Spirit in my heart,
  That I may live for thee.

Henry Ernest Hardy

Christ my all

My God, accept my heart this day,
    And make it always thine,
That I from thee no more may stray,
    No more from thee decline.

Before the cross of him who died,
    Behold, I prostrate fall;
Let every sin be crucified,
    And Christ be all in all.

Let every thought and work and word
    To thee be ever given;
Then life shall be thy service, Lord,
    And death the gate of heaven.

Matthew Bridges

All for Christ

Lord, in the strength of grace,
    With a glad heart and free,
Myself, my residue of days,
    I consecrate to thee.

Thy ransomed servant, I
    Restore to thee thine own;
And, from this moment, live or die
    To serve my God alone.

Charles Wesley

So rich a crown

When I survey the wondrous cross,
  On which the Prince of Glory died,
My richest gain I count but loss,
  And pour contempt on all my pride.

Forbid it, Lord, that I should boast
  Save in the death of Christ my God;
All the vain things that charm me most,
  I sacrifice them to his blood.

See from his head, his hands, his feet,
  Sorrow and love flow mingled down;
Did e'er such love and sorrow meet,
  Or thorns compose so rich a crown?

His dying crimson, like a robe,
  Spreads o'er his body on the tree;
Then am I dead to all the globe,
  And all the globe is dead to me.

Were the whole realm of nature mine,
  That were a present far too small;
Love so amazing, so divine,
  Demands my soul, my life, my all.

Isaac Watts

5. NEITHER LIFE NOR DEATH
The pilgrim way

Morning – Today with God
The day's work – The narrow way
In temptation – Strength and courage
Faith and healing – To make Christ known
Close of day – Fear of death
No darker rooms – Life eternal
Christ at the last

O Lord, who thy dear life didst give
For us in narrow grave to lie,
Teach us to die that we may live,
To live that we may never die.

Cecil Frances Alexander

At sunrise

Christ, whose glory fills the skies,
   Christ, the true, the only Light,
Sun of Righteousness, arise,
   Triumph o'er the shades of night;
Day-spring from on high, be near;
Day-star, in my heart appear.

Dark and cheerless is the morn
   Unaccompanied by thee:
Joyless is the day's return,
   Till thy mercy's beams I see,
Till they inward light impart,
Glad my eyes, and warm my heart.

Visit then this soul of mine;
   Pierce the gloom of sin and grief;
Fill me, radiancy divine;
   Scatter all my unbelief;
More and more thyself display,
Shining to the perfect day.

Charles Wesley

God of the morning

God of the morning, at whose voice
The cheerful sun makes haste to rise,
And like a giant doth rejoice
To run his journey through the skies;

O, like the sun, may I fulfil
The appointed duties of the day,
With ready mind and active will
March on and keep my heavenly way.

Isaac Watts

Today with God

I bind unto myself today
   The power of God to hold and lead,
His eye to watch, his might to stay,
   His ear to hearken to my need,
The wisdom of my God to teach,
   His hand to guide, his shield to ward,
The word of God to give me speech,
   His heavenly host to be my guard.

Christ be with me, Christ within me,
   Christ behind me, Christ before me,
Christ beside me, Christ to win me,
   Christ to comfort and restore me,
Christ beneath me, Christ above me,
   Christ in quiet, Christ in danger,
Christ in hearts of all that love me,
   Christ in mouth of friend and stranger.

St Patrick
translated by Cecil Frances Alexander

The day's work

Forth in thy name, O Lord, I go,
My daily labour to pursue,
Thee, only thee, resolved to know
In all I think, or speak, or do.

The task thy wisdom has assigned
O let me cheerfully fulfil,
In all my works thy presence find,
And prove thy good and perfect will.

Thee may I set at my right hand,
Whose eyes my inmost substance see,
And labour on at thy command,
And offer all my works to thee.

Give me to bear thy easy yoke,
And every moment watch and pray,
And still to things eternal look,
And hasten to thy glorious day;

For thee delightfully employ
Whate'er thy bounteous grace has given,
And run my course with even joy,
And closely walk with thee to heaven.

Charles Wesley

Strength for today

Great is thy faithfulness, O God my Father,
There is no shadow of turning with thee:
Thou changest not, thy compassions they fail not.
As thou hast been, thou for ever wilt be.

Great is thy faithfulness, O God my Father,
Morning by morning new mercies I see;
All I have needed thy hand hath provided.
Great is thy faithfulness, Lord, unto me.

Thomas Obediah Chisholm

A day at a time

Tomorrow, Lord, is thine,
　Lodged in thy sovereign hand,
And if its sun arise and shine,
　It shines by thy command.

The present moment flies,
　And bears our life away;
O make thy servants truly wise,
　That they may live today.

Philip Doddridge

The narrow way

Thy way, not mine, O Lord,
However dark it be:
Lead me by thine own hand,
Choose out the path for me.

The kingdom that I seek
Is thine: so let the way
That leads to it be thine,
Else I must surely stray.

Take thou my cup, and it
With joy or sorrow fill,
As best to thee may seem;
Choose thou my good and ill.

Not mine, not mine the choice
In things or great or small;
Be thou my guide, my strength,
My wisdom and my all.

Horatius Bonar

'Who keepeth thee'

Unto the hills around do I lift up
   My longing eyes.
O whence for me shall my salvation come,
   From whence arise?
From God the Lord doth come my certain aid,
From God the Lord, who heaven and earth hath
    made.

Jehovah is himself thy keeper true,
   Thy changeless shade.
Jehovah thy defence on thy right hand
   Himself hath made.
And thee no sun by day shall ever smite,
No moon shall harm thee in the silent night.

From every evil shall he keep thy soul,
   From every sin;
Jehovah shall preserve thy going out,
   Thy coming in.
Above thee watching, he, whom we adore,
Shall keep thee henceforth, yea, for evermore.

John Douglas Sutherland Campbell

In temptation

Jesu, Lover of my soul
   Let me to thy bosom fly,
While the nearer waters roll,
   While the tempest still is high;
Hide me, O my Saviour, hide,
   Till the storm of life is past;
Safe into the haven guide,
   O receive my soul at last!

Other refuge have I none,
   Hangs my helpless soul on thee;
Leave, ah, leave me not alone,
   Still support and comfort me.
All my trust on thee is stayed,
   All my help from thee I bring;
Cover my defenceless head
   With the shadow of thy wing.

Charles Wesley

The storms of life

In suffering, be thy love my peace,
In weakness, be thy love my power;
And when the storms of life shall cease,
Jesus, in that tremendous hour,
In death as life be thou my guide,
And save me, who for me hast died.

Paulus Gerhardt
translated by John Wesley

Strength and courage

Father, hear the prayer we offer:
   Not for ease that prayer shall be,
But for strength that we may ever
   Live our lives courageously.

Not for ever in green pastures
   Do we ask our way to be;
But the steep and rugged pathway
   May we tread rejoicingly.

Love Maria Willis

Faith and healing

Here, Master, in this quiet place,
Where anyone may kneel,
I also come to ask for grace,
Believing you can heal.

If pain of body, stress of mind,
Destroys my inward peace,
In prayer for others may I find
The secret of release.

If self upon its sickness feeds
And turns my life to gall,
Let me not brood upon my needs,
But simply tell you all.

You never said 'You ask too much'
To any troubled soul.
I long to feel your healing touch –
Will you not make me whole?

But if the thing I most desire
Is not your way for me,
May faith, when tested in the fire,
Prove its integrity.

Of all my prayers, may this be chief:
Till faith is fully grown,
Lord, disbelieve my unbelief,
And claim me as your own.

Frederick Pratt Green

Caring and sharing

Lord Christ, who on thy heart didst bear
   The burden of our shame and sin,
And now on high dost stoop to share
   The fight without, the fear within;

Thy patience cannot know defeat,
   Thy pity will not be denied,
Thy loving-kindness still is great,
   Thy tender mercies still abide.

So in our present need we pray
   To thee, our living, healing Lord,
That we thy people, day by day,
   May follow thee and keep thy word;

That we may care, as thou hast cared,
   For sick and lame, for deaf and blind,
And freely share, as thou hast shared,
   In all the sorrows of mankind.

Henry Arnold Thomas

To make Christ known

Facing a task unfinished,
That drives us to our knees,
A need that, undiminished,
Rebukes our slothful ease,
We, who rejoice to know thee,
Renew before thy throne
The solemn pledge we owe thee
To go and make thee known.

We bear the torch that flaming
Fell from the hands of those
Who gave their lives proclaiming
That Jesus died and rose.
Ours is the same commission,
The same glad message ours.
Fired by the same ambition,
To thee we yield our powers.

O Father who sustained them,
O Spirit who inspired,
Saviour, whose love constrained them
To toil with zeal untired,
From cowardice defend us,
From lethargy awake!
Forth on thine errands send us
To labour for thy sake.

Frank Houghton

Evening prayer

God, that madest earth and heaven,
    Darkness and light,
Who the day for toil hast given,
    For rest the night,
May thine angel-guards defend us,
Slumber sweet thy mercy send us,
Holy dreams and hopes attend us,
    This livelong night.

Guard us waking, guard us sleeping;
    And, when we die,
May we in thy mighty keeping
    All peaceful lie.
When the last dread call shall wake us,
Do not thou, our God, forsake us,
But to reign in glory take us
    With thee on high.

Reginald Heber and Richard Whately

Against all perils

Grant us thy peace, Lord, through the coming
    night;
Turn thou for us its darkness into light;
From harm and danger keep thy children free;
For dark and light are both alike to thee.

John Ellerton

Before sleep

Glory to thee, my God, this night
For all the blessings of the light;
Keep me, O keep me, King of kings,
Beneath thine own almighty wings.

Forgive me, Lord, for thy dear Son,
The ill that I this day have done,
That with the world, myself, and thee,
I, ere I sleep, at peace may be.

Teach me to live, that I may dread
The grave as little as my bed;
Teach me to die, that so I may
Rise glorious at the aweful day.

Thomas Ken

Close of day

Sun of my soul, thou Saviour dear,
It is not night if thou be near;
O may no earth-born cloud arise
To hide thee from thy servant's eyes!

When the soft dews of kindly sleep
My wearied eyelids gently steep,
Be my last thought: how sweet to rest
For ever on my Saviour's breast!

Abide with me from morn till eve,
For without thee I cannot live;
Abide with me when night is nigh,
For without thee I dare not die.

If some poor wandering child of thine
Have spurned today the voice divine,
Now, Lord, the gracious work begin;
Let him no more lie down in sin.

Watch by the sick; enrich the poor
With blessings from thy boundless store;
Be every mourner's sleep tonight
Like infant's slumbers, pure and light.

Come near and bless us when we wake,
Ere through the world our way we take,
Till in the ocean of thy love
We lose ourselves in heaven above.

John Keble

Fear of death

I said sometimes with tears,
Ah me! I'm loth to die.
Lord! Silence thou those fears:
My life's with thee on high.
    Sweet truth to me!
    I shall arise
    And with these eyes
    My Saviour see.

Samuel Crossman

Living and dying

Today I live, but once shall come my death;
One day shall still my laughter and my crying,
Bring to a halt my heart-beat and my breath:
Lord, give me faith for living and for dying.

How I shall die, or when, I do not know,
Nor where, for endless is the world's horizon;
But save me, Lord, from thoughts that lay me low,
From morbid fears that freeze my power of reason.

When earthly life shall close, as close it must,
Let Jesus be my brother and my merit.
Let me without regret recall the past,
Then, Lord, into your hands commit my spirit.

Meanwhile I live and move and I am glad,
Enjoy this life and all its interweaving:
Each given day, as I take up the thread,
Let love suggest my mode, my mood of living.

Frederik Herman Kaan

No darker rooms

Lord, it belongs not to my care
    Whether I die or live;
To love and serve thee is my share,
    And this thy grace must give.

If life be long, I will be glad
    That I may long obey;
If short, yet why should I be sad
    To soar to endless day?

Christ leads me through no darker rooms
    Than he went through before;
He that into God's kingdom comes
    Must enter by this door.

Come, Lord, when grace has made me meet
    Thy blessèd face to see;
For if thy work on earth be sweet,
    What will thy glory be!

My knowledge of that life is small,
    The eye of faith is dim;
But 'tis enough that Christ knows all,
    And I shall be with him.

Richard Baxter

Life eternal

Now is eternal life,
　　If risen with Christ we stand,
　In him to life reborn,
　　And holden in his hand;
No more we fear death's ancient dread,
In Christ arisen from the dead.

Unfathomed love divine,
　　Reign thou within my heart;
　From thee nor depth nor height,
　　Nor life nor death can part;
My life is hid in God with thee,
Now and through all eternity.

George Wallace Briggs

Christ at the last

Abide with me; fast falls the eventide;
The darkness deepens; Lord, with me abide;
When other helpers fail, and comforts flee,
Help of the helpless, O abide with me.

I need thy presence every passing hour;
What but thy grace can foil the tempter's power?
Who like thyself my guide and stay can be?
Through cloud and sunshine, O abide with me.

Hold thou thy cross before my closing eyes;
Shine through the gloom, and point me to the
    skies;
Heaven's morning breaks, and earth's vain
    shadows flee;
In life, in death, O Lord, abide with me!

Henry Francis Lyte

6. GOD'S NEW BEST NAME
Love beyond all telling

By love, for love – Wonder, love and praise
Love is the lesson – Joy in love
Growing in grace – The single eye
Clinging to Christ – God cares
The greatest of these – The God of peace
God my all

Into the love of God, I pray,
Deeper and deeper let me press,
Exploring all along the way
Its hidden strength and tenderness.

Into the steadfastness of one
Who patiently endured the cross,
Of him who, though he were a son,
Came to his crown through bitter loss.

This is the road of my desire –
Learning to love as God loves me,
Ready to pass through flood or fire
With Christ's unwearying constancy.

Frank Houghton

By love, for love

Great God, your love has called us here
  As we, by love, for love were made;
Your living likeness still we bear,
  Though marred, dishonoured, disobeyed;
We come, with all our heart and mind,
Your call to hear, your love to find.

We come with self-inflicted pains
  Of broken trust and chosen wrong,
Half-free, half-bound by inner chains,
  By social forces swept along,
By powers and systems close confined,
Yet seeking hope for humankind.

Great God, in Christ you call our name,
  And then receive us as your own,
Not through some merit, right or claim,
  But by your gracious love alone;
We strain to glimpse your mercy-seat,
And find you kneeling at our feet.

Then take the towel, and break the bread,
  And humble us, and call us friends;
Suffer and serve till all are fed,
  And show how grandly love intends
To work till all creation sings,
To fill all worlds, to crown all things.

Great God, in Christ you set us free
  Your life to live, your joy to share;
Give us your Spirit's liberty
  To turn from guilt and dull despair
And offer all that faith can do,
While love is making all things new.

Brian Arthur Wren

All for love's sake

Thou who wast rich beyond all splendour,
All for love's sake becamest poor;
Thrones for a manger didst surrender,
Sapphire-paved courts for stable floor.
Thou who wast rich beyond all splendour,
All for love's sake becamest poor.

Thou who art God beyond all praising,
All for love's sake becamest man;
Stooping so low, but sinners raising
Heavenwards by thine eternal plan.
Thou who art God beyond all praising,
All for love's sake becamest man.

Thou who art love beyond all telling,
Saviour and King, we worship thee.
Emmanuel, within us dwelling,
Make us what thou wouldst have us be.
Thou who art love beyond all telling,
Saviour and King, we worship thee.

Frank Houghton

Wonder, love and praise

Love divine, all loves excelling,
   Joy of heaven to earth come down,
Fix in us thy humble dwelling,
   All thy faithful mercies crown.
Jesu, thou art all compassion,
   Pure, unbounded love thou art;
Visit us with thy salvation,
   Enter every trembling heart.

Come, almighty to deliver,
   Let us all thy life receive;
Suddenly return, and never,
   Never more thy temples leave.
Thee we would be always blessing,
   Serve thee as thy hosts above,
Pray, and praise thee, without ceasing,
   Glory in thy perfect love.

Finish then thy new creation,
   Pure and spotless let us be;
Let us see thy great salvation,
   Perfectly restored in thee.
Changed from glory into glory,
   Till in heaven we take our place,
Till we cast our crowns before thee,
   Lost in wonder, love, and praise!

Charles Wesley

Love is the lesson

Most glorious Lord of life, that on this day
Didst make thy triumph over death and sin
And, having harrowed hell, didst bring away
Captivity thence captive, us to win:

This joyous day, dear Lord, with joy begin;
And grant that we, for whom thou didest die,
Being with thy dear blood clean washt from sin,
May live for ever in felicity;

And that thy love we weighing worthily,
May likewise love thee for the same again;
And for thy sake, that all like dear didst buy,
With love may one another entertain.

So let us love, dear Love, like as we ought:
Love is the lesson which the Lord us taught.

Edmund Spenser

By love inflamed

Father, who didst fashion me
Image of thyself to be,
Fill me with thy love divine,
Let my every thought be thine.

Holy Jesus, may I be
Dead and buried here with thee;
And, by love inflamed, arise
Unto thee a sacrifice.

Thou who dost all gifts impart,
Shine, blest Spirit, in my heart;
Best of gifts, thyself bestow;
Make me burn thy love to know.

from the Latin of the Carcasson
Breviary, 1745, translated by
Henry Williams Baker

Joy in love

Come, my Way, my Truth, my Life:
   Such a Way, as gives us breath;
   Such a Truth, as ends all strife;
   Such a Life, as killeth death.

Come, my Light, my Feast, my Strength:
   Such a Light, as shows a feast;
   Such a Feast, as mends in length;
   Such a Strength, as makes his guest.

Come, my Joy, my Love, my Heart:
   Such a Joy, as none can move;
   Such a Love, as none can part;
   Such a Heart, as joys in love.

George Herbert

Growing in grace

O Jesus Christ, grow thou in me,
  And all things else recede;
My heart be daily nearer thee,
  From sin be daily freed.

More of thy glory let me see,
  Thou holy, wise, and true!
I would thy living image be,
  In joy and sorrow too.

Fill me with gladness from above,
  Hold me by strength divine!
Lord, let the glow of thy great love
  Through my whole being shine.

Make this poor self grow less and less,
  Be thou my life and aim;
O make me daily, through thy grace,
  More meet to bear thy name!

Johann Caspar Lavater
translated by Elizabeth Lee Smith

The single eye

God of almighty love,
    By whose sufficient grace
I lift my heart to things above,
    And humbly seek thy face:

Whate'er I say or do,
    Thy glory be my aim;
My offerings all be offered through
    The ever-blessèd name.

Jesus, my single eye
    Be fixed on thee alone:
Thy name be praised on earth, on high,
    Thy will by all be done.

Charles Wesley

Clinging to Christ

None other lamb, none other name,
   None other hope in heaven or earth or sea,
None other hiding-place from guilt and shame,
   None beside thee!

My faith burns low, my hope burns low;
   Only my heart's desire cries out in me,
By the deep thunder of its want and woe,
   Cries out to thee.

Lord, thou art life, though I be dead;
   Love's fire thou art, however cold I be:
Nor heaven have I, nor place to lay my head,
   Nor home, but thee.

Christina Georgina Rossetti

The praise of his glory

King of Glory, King of Peace,
   I will love thee;
And that love may never cease
   I will move thee.
Thou hast granted my request,
   Thou hast heard me;
Thou didst note my working breast,
   Thou hast spared me.

Wherefore with my utmost art
   I will sing thee,
And the cream of all my heart
   I will bring thee.
Though my sins against me cried,
   Thou didst clear me;
And alone, when they replied,
   Thou didst hear me.

Seven whole days, not one in seven,
   I will praise thee;
In my heart, though not in heaven,
   I can raise thee.
Small it is, in this poor sort
   To enrol thee:
E'en eternity's too short
   To extol thee.

George Herbert

God cares

God, who made the earth,
The air, the sky, the sea,
Who gave the light its birth,
Careth for me.

God, who made the sun,
The moon, the stars, is he
Who, when life's clouds come on,
Careth for me.

God, who sent his Son
To die on Calvary,
He, if I lean on him,
Will care for me.

Sarah Betts Rhodes

'Feed my lambs'

Help me, Lord, to feed and keep
First the lambs, and then the sheep,
Lambs to make my tenderest care,
Lambs within my arms to bear:
Both my happy charge I make,
Both I cherish for thy sake,
Thus in life, and death, to prove,
Loved of thee, that thee I love.

Charles Wesley

The greatest of these

Love is kind and suffers long,
Love is meek and thinks no wrong,
Love than death itself more strong;
   Therefore give us love.

Faith will vanish into sight;
Hope be emptied in delight;
Love in heaven will shine more bright;
   Therefore give us love.

Christopher Wordsworth

The God of peace

For peace with God above
  And every sin forgiven,
  For all our hope of heaven,
We lift our hearts in love.

The peace of God be ours
  Enfolding every part,
  Possessing thought and heart,
The will and all its powers.

The God of peace defend
  And keep us all our days
  Unwearied in his praise,
Whose peace shall never end.

Timothy Dudley-Smith

God my all

God be in my head, and in my understanding;
God be in mine eyes, and in my looking;
God be in my mouth, and in my speaking;
God be in my heart, and in my thinking;
God be at mine end, and at my departing.

Anonymous
from a Book of Hours, 1514

EPILOGUE

Vespers

When I have said my quiet say,
When I have sung my little song,
How sweetly, sweetly dies the day,
The valley and the hill along;
How sweet the summons, 'Come away'
That calls me from the busy throng!

I thought beside the water's flow
Awhile to lie beneath the leaves,
I thought in Autumn's harvest glow
To rest my head upon the sheaves;
But lo! methinks the day was brief
And cloudy; flower, nor fruit nor leaf
I bring, and yet accepted, free
And blest, my Lord, I come to thee.

What matter now for promise lost
Through blast of spring or summer rains!
What matter now for purpose crost,
For broken hopes and wasted pains!
What if the olive little yields!
What if the grape be blighted! Thine
The corn upon a thousand fields,
Upon a thousand hills the vine.

My spirit bare before thee stands;
I bring no gift, I ask no sign,
I come to thee with empty hands,
The surer to be filled from thine.

Dora Greenwell

Acknowledgements

Every effort has been made to trace the copyright holders of the material quoted in this book. Information on any omissions should be communicated to the publishers, who will make full acknowledgements in future editions.

The compiler and publishers are pleased to acknowledge the following for permission to quote their copyright material:

The Revd Brian Foley for 'Lord, as I wake I turn to you'.

Hope Publishing Company for 'Great is thy faithfulness' and 'Saviour, I seek your face'.

Jubilate Hymns for 'Lord, you need no house' and 'O Master Christ, draw near to take'.

Mowbray/Cassell plc for 'O dearest Lord, thy sacred head'.

Lady Mynors for 'Lord of all, to whom alone'.

OMF Books for 'Facing a task unfinished', 'Into the love of God, I pray' and 'Thou who wast rich beyond all splendour'.

Oxford University Press for 'Lord of the house', 'Come, risen Lord', 'Now is eternal life' and 'Lord God, your love has called us here'.

The Revd Prof Charles Price for 'Lord, for ever at thy side'.

Stainer and Bell Ltd for 'Here, Master, in this quiet place' and 'Today I live, but once shall come my death'.

Index of hymn writers

An asterisk after the name indicates an entry in the *Dictionary of National Biography*.

ALEXANDER*, Cecil Frances (1818–95). Née Humphreys, married in 1850 William Alexander who became Bishop of Derry and Raphoe, Ireland, 1867; and Primate from 1893. Her *Hymns for Little Children*, 1848 saw over 100 editions. 63, 81, 85

ALINGTON*, Cyril Argentine (1872–1955). Ordained in 1899, he was appointed headmaster of Shrewsbury School, 1908; and of Eton College, 1916; becoming Dean of Durham, 1933–51. 33

ANDREW, Father – see HARDY, Henry Ernest

ANONYMOUS 21, 43, 44, 69, 113, 123

BAKER*, Sir Henry Williams, Bart. (1821–77). Ordained in 1844, he was vicar of Monkland, Herefordshire from 1851 until his death. First chairman of *Hymns Ancient and Modern*, to which he contributed translations and original texts. 113

BAXTER*, Richard (1615–91). Ordained 1638 and a regimental chaplain during the Civil War, later becoming a nonconformist minister and puritan divine. Author of *The Saints' Everlasting Rest*, 1650. 103

BAYLY, Albert Frederick (1901–84). Ordained 1929 to the Congregational ministry; and among the earliest contributors to the post-war 'hymn explosion', publishing four collections of his hymn texts. 52

BENNETT, Lucy Ann (1850–1927). Born, lived and died in the Falfield area of Gloucestershire, and for nearly fifty years Secretary of Mount Pleasant Chapel. Though frail in health, she published, among other writings, three volumes of verse and hymns. 27

BIANCO DA SIENA, died 1434 in Venice. As a young man he entered a lay religious Order. His collected hymns were published in 1851. 3

BONAR*, Horatius (1808–89). Ordained in 1837 but at the Great Disruption of 1843 he helped to found the Free Church of Scotland; and in 1883 was elected Moderator of its General Assembly. He wrote in all some 600 hymns. 7, 15, 38, 89

BRIDGES, Matthew (1800–94). Writer. He turned Roman Catholic in middle life and after a period in Canada lived (and died) at the Convent of the Assumption, Sidmouth, Devon. 77

BRIDGES*, Robert Seymour (1844–1930). Qualified as a doctor in 1874 but soon relinquished medicine for literature and music, becoming Poet Laureate in 1913. Published the influential *Yattendon Hymnal*, 1899. 25

BRIGGS, George Wallace (1875–1959). Ordained in 1889, he became Canon of Worcester, 1924 and of Leicester, 1927. He was closely associated with *Songs of Praise*, 1926; and published his collected texts as *Songs of Faith*, 1945. 18, 104

BRIGHT*, William (1824–1901). Ordained in 1848, he became Regius Professor of Ecclesiastical History and Canon of Christ Church, Oxford from 1868. 19

BYRNE, Mary Elizabeth (1880–1931). Erse scholar and researcher, and assistant editor of the *Dictionary of the Irish Language*. 43

CAMPBELL, John Douglas Sutherland, 9th Duke of Argyll (1845–1914). A Member of Parliament 1868–78 and 1898–1900, and Governor-General of Canada 1878–83. He married Princess Louise, fourth daughter of Queen Victoria, and succeeded to the title in 1900. 90

CHATFIELD, Allen William (1808–96). Ordained in 1832, he remained vicar of Much Marcle, Herefordshire, from 1848 to his death. He published many verse translations of early Greek Christian writings. 23

CHISHOLM, Thomas Obediah (1866–1960). American. Teacher, journalist and briefly a Methodist minister, he wrote over a thousand hymns. 87

CLARKSON, Edith Margaret (1915–   ). Canadian. Poet, teacher, author and widely-published hymn writer, her collected texts appeared as *A Singing Heart*, 1987. 20

CONDER*, Josiah (1789–1855). Writer, bookseller, editor and poet, he compiled the *Congregational Hymn Book*, 1836. 6

COWPER*, William (1731–1800). After a legal training he became a writer and distinguished minor poet, though subject to severe depressive illness. With John Newton (q.v.) he wrote *Olney Hymns*, 1779. 39

CROLY*, George (1780–1860). Born and ordained in Ireland, but beneficed in London c.1810. Writer, dramatic critic, poet; and editor of *Hymns and Psalms for Public Worship*, 1854. 4

CROSSMAN*, Samuel (c.1624–1683). After a period of nonconformist ministry he was episcopally ordained in 1665. From 1682 he served as Treasurer of Bristol Cathedral, becoming Dean in 1683. 101

DEARMER*, Percy (1867–1936). Ordained in 1891, he was appointed Professor of Ecclesiastical Art at King's College, London, 1919, and Canon of Westminster, 1931. A writer of hymns himself, he was joint editor of the *English Hymnal*, 1906 and *Songs of Praise*, 1926. 21

DODDRIDGE*, Philip (1702–51). Teacher, pastor and Congregational minister, his best known work is *The Rise and Progress of Religion in the Soul*, 1745. He wrote some 400 hymns. 88

DUDLEY-SMITH, Timothy (1926–). Ordained in 1950, becoming suffragan Bishop of Thetford, Norfolk, in 1981. His collected hymns are currently published as *Lift Every Heart*, 1984 and *Songs of Deliverance*, 1988. 122

ELLERTON, John (1826–93). Ordained in 1850, he began to write hymns during eight years as curate in Brighton. A hymnologist and hymnal editor, his collected texts were published as *Hymns Original and Translated*, 1888. 98

ELLIOTT*, Charlotte (1789–1871). A permanent invalid following a serious illness in 1821, she wrote much religious verse including some 150 hymns. 35

FOLEY, William Brian (1919–). Ordained in 1945, he serves as Roman Catholic parish priest in Clayton Green, Chorley, Lancashire; and was a considerable contributor to the *New Catholic Hymnal*, 1971 and subsequent major hymnals. 46

GERHARDT, Paulus (1607–76). Ordained to the Lutheran ministry in 1651, he became in 1669 archdiaconus of Luben. His 134 hymns found favour from the first and many are still widely used, especially in his native Germany. 25, 72, 92

GREEN, Frederick Pratt (1903–). Ordained to the Methodist ministry in 1928 and widely known as a poet and playwright, his hymns appear in almost every contemporary hymnal and are collected in *The Hymns and Ballads of Fred Pratt Green*, 1982. 94

GREENWELL*, Dora (1821–82). Author, minor poet and distinguished devotional writer, she published prose works including biography and several collections of religious verse. 125

HARDY, Henry Ernest (1869–1946). Ordained in 1894, he founded the Society of the Divine Compassion and worked for fifty years in Plaistow, East London, as 'Father Andrew'. 76

HART*, Joseph (1712–68). From 1759 Minister at Jewin Street Independent Chapel, London. His many hymns were among the most widely sung of his generation. 1

HATCH*, Edwin (1835–89). Ordained in 1859, after a Professorship in Toronto he became Reader in Ecclesiastical History at Oxford, 1886. His hymns were collected posthumously in *Towards Fields of Light*, 1890. 71

HAVERGAL*, Frances Ridley (1836–79). An accomplished linguist and musician, of indifferent health but fervent spirituality. She wrote both texts and tunes in a variety of journals, leaflets and collections. 50, 57, 75

HEBER*, Reginald (1783–1826). Ordained in 1807, he became Bishop of Calcutta in 1823, having twice declined. His hymns were mostly written early in his ministry, and only published after his early death. 10, 97

HERBERT*, George (1593–1633). Public Orator of Cambridge in 1619 and ordained in 1626, he was noted for his poems and writings and as the saintly Rector of Bemerton, a tiny parish near Salisbury. His advice to the rural parson, *A Priest to the Temple*, appeared posthumously in his *Remains*, 1652. 47, 114, 118

HOLROYDE, James (1850–1933). Ordained in 1873, he served curacies in Liverpool, London and Staffordshire. For twenty-five years he was vicar of Stapleford, Nottingham; and of Patcham, Sussex, from 1915 to his death. His name sometimes appears without the final E. 58

HOUGHTON, Frank (1894–1972). Ordained in 1917, he was

consecrated Bishop of East Szachwan, China, in 1937. From 1940–51 he was General Director of the China Inland Mission. 96, 107, 110

HOW*, William Walsham (1823–97). Ordained in 1846 and consecrated 1879 as Bishop of Bedford (for East London), he was translated in 1888 to be first Bishop of Wakefield. Starting as a schoolboy he wrote some sixty hymns. 16

HULL, Eleanor Henrietta (1860–1935). An expert in Irish art, culture, literature and folklore, she was founder of the Irish Text Society. 43

HUMPHREYS, Charles William (1840–1921). An insurance manager, his best known hymns are translations for the *English Hymnal*, 1906. 21

IDLE, Christopher Martin (1938–   ). Ordained in 1965, for twelve years Rector of Limehouse, East London, and now a country parson in Suffolk. A contributor to many hymnals, he has edited *Anglican Praise*, 1987 and the quarterly *News of Hymnody*. 68

KAAN, Frederik Herman, (1929–   ). Born and educated in the Netherlands, he was ordained to the Congregational ministry in the UK in 1955 and served pastorates until 1968. After ten years of ecumenical ministry in Geneva he became a Provincial Moderator in the United Reformed Church in the UK, 1978–85; followed by ecumenical ministry in Swindon. His hymns are collected in *The Hymn Texts of Fred Kaan*, 1985 and *Planting Trees and Sowing Seeds*, 1989. 102

KEBLE*, John (1792–1866). Fellow of Oriel College, Oxford, in 1811, he was ordained in 1815 and from 1836–63 was Vicar of Hursley. A notable figure of the Oxford Movement, his *The Christian Year*, 1827 went through ninety-two editions in his lifetime. Keble College, Oxford commemorates him. 44, 100

KEN*, Thomas (1637–1711). Ordained in 1661 and consecrated Bishop of Bath and Wells in 1685, he was deprived as a non-juror in 1691. His posthumous *Poems* in four volumes include *Hymns for all the Festivals of the Year*. 99

LATHBURY, Mary Artemisia (1841–1913). American. A professional artist, writer and editor, associated with the Chautauqua Assembly in New York State for which the hymn 'Break thou the bread of life' was originally written. 59

LAVATER, Johann Caspar (1741–1801). Ordained 1762 as a minister of the Reformed Church of Switzerland, he became pastor of two Zurich churches and wrote some 700 hymns. 115

LITTLEDALE*, Richard Frederick (1833–90). Irish by descent, he was ordained in 1856 and published some fifty books including hymns translated from seven or eight languages together with original compositions. 3

LUTHER, Martin (1483–1546). Ordained 1507 and lecturer in the University of Wittenberg, 1508. In 1517 he posted his 95 theses on the door of the Castle Church, and was excommunicated in 1521. The founder of the German Reformation and the Church that bears his name, to which he bequeathed a strong tradition of hymnody. 67

LYTE*, Henry Francis (1793–1847). Born in Scotland and educated in Ireland, he was ordained in 1815 and served from 1823 as perpetual curate of Lower Brixham, Devon. He wrote much hymnody and verse; and edited the poems of Henry Vaughan. 26, 105

MATHESON*, George (1842–1906). He was ordained into the ministry of the Church of Scotland, 1866; and became Fellow of the Royal Society of Edinburgh, 1890. Almost blind from youth, he published considerable theological works, and *Sacred Songs*, 1890. 73

MONSELL*, John Samuel Bewley (1811–75). Ordained in 1834, he ministered in Surrey parishes and published eleven volumes of verse, including some 300 hymns. 29

MONTGOMERY*, James (1771–1854). For thirty-one years a Sheffield newspaper proprietor and editor, he wrote over 400 highly-regarded hymns, and is considered among the greatest English lay hymn writers. 12, 13, 14, 17, 37, 54, 56

MOULE*, Handley Carr Glyn (1841–1920). Fellow of Trinity College, Cambridge, 1865 and ordained 1867, he became first Principal of Ridley Hall, Cambridge in 1881 and Professor of Divinity 1889, before being consecrated Bishop of Durham in 1901. 65

MOWBRAY, David (1938–). Ordained in 1963, serving parishes in Northampton, Watford, Broxbourne and Hertford, he has published privately three collections of his hymns: *Kingdom Come*, 1978; *Kingdom Everlasting*, 1980; and *Kingdom Within*, 1984. 48

NEWTON*, John (1725–1807). After service in the Navy and as a slave trader, he was ordained in 1964 as curate of Olney, Buckinghamshire, where with Cowper (q.v.) he produced *Olney Hymns*, 1789. As rector of St Mary Woolnoth in the City of London from 1780 he was of much service to William Wilberforce in the fight against slavery. 28, 61

PALMER, Ray (1808–87). American. Ordained in 1835 to a Congregational pastorate in Maine, he became Corresponding Secretary of the American Congregational Union, 1865–78. He is especially noted as a translator of hymns. 34, 69, 70

PATRICK*, Saint (c.373–c.463). Patron Saint of Ireland, having been captured at the age of sixteen and taken there as a slave. Ordained c.417 and consecrated bishop in 432, he founded the Cathedral Church of Armagh in 444. 85

PRICE, Charles Philip (1920–   ). American. Ordained in 1949, later becoming Preacher to the University at Harvard and Professor of Systematic Theology at Virginia Seminary. An author, hymn writer and translator, he was co-chairman of the text committee for *The Hymnal 1982* of the American Episcopal Church. 54

PROCTOR*, Adelaide Anne (1825–64). Charles Dickens published her first poems, and paid tribute to her work among London's poor. A convert to Roman Catholicism, her poems appeared as *Legends and Lyrics*, 1858. 9

RHODES, Sarah Betts (1829–1904). Née Bradshaw, she married a master silversmith in Sheffield and after his death became headmistress of a girls' school in Worksop. 119

RINKART, Martin (1586–1649). In 1611 he became diaconus in Eisleben, Germany. Six years later he was made Archdeacon of Eilenburg where he served through most of the Thirty Years' War. 11

ROSSETTI*, Christina Georgina (1830–94). Daughter of the Professor of Italian at London University and sister of Dante Gabriel, she was a considerable Christian poet though for many years an invalid. 66, 117

SMITH, Elizabeth Lee (1817–98). American, née Allen. Daughter of the President of Dartmouth University, her husband was Professor at Union Theological Seminary, New York. A linguist and translator, she was recognised as a gifted writer in her day. 115

SPENSER*, Edmund (c.1552–99). After an appointment in the household of the Earl of Leicester he settled in 1586 at the Castle of Kilcolman, Co. Cork, engaging in literary work and preparing his great poem *The Faerie Queene* for the press. He died in penury and is buried in Westminster Abbey. 112

STEELE*, Anne (1717–78). Daughter of a Baptist lay pastor at Broughton, Hampshire, and of delicate health, she published some 150 hymns and was regarded as a major hymn writer of her time. 55

SYNESIUS (c.373–430). A native of Cyrene, neoplatonist, philosopher, musician and statesman. From a pagan upbringing he was converted to Christ and in 410 consecrated Bishop of Ptolemais in northern Greece. Of his *Ten Odes*, this alone is sung as a hymn. 23

THOMAS, Henry Arnold (1848–1924). He was for forty years minister of Highbury Congregational Church, Bristol; and in 1899 Chairman of the Congregational Union of England and Wales. 95

TOPLADY*, Augustus Montague (1740–78). Ordained in 1762, he was first a friend and then a foe of John Wesley, becoming a fierce and noted controversialist. Of his 133 hymns, 'Rock of Ages' is still in universal use. 31

TUTTIETT, Lawrence (1825–97). Ordained in 1848, he became minister of the Episcopal church of St Andrews, Scotland in 1870; and in 1877 Canon of St Ninian's Cathedral, Perth. Among his many devotional writings he published two volumes of hymns. 45

WATTS*, Isaac (1674–1748). Ordained in 1702 as an independent minister, he was also domestic chaplain, educationalist, author and (pre-eminently) hymn writer. He is widely regarded as 'the father of English hymnody'. 5, 8, 53, 79, 84

WESLEY*, Charles (1707–88). Younger brother to John, ordained 1735, perhaps 'the first Methodist' and, with Isaac Watts, England's greatest hymn writer. His contribution to the

Methodist Revival is second only to his brother's. xv, 30, 32, 36, 51, 64, 74, 78, 83, 86, 91, 111, 116, 120

WESLEY*, John (1703–91). Ordained in 1725, he became the founder of Methodism, enduring immense opposition, travelling vast distances, and preaching some 40,000 sermons. In hymnody he excelled as translator and editor. 72, 92

WHATELY*, Richard (1787–1863). Ordained in 1814 as tutor of Oriel College, Oxford where in 1929 he became Professor of Political Economy. He was consecrated Archbishop of Dublin in 1831. 97

WHITTIER, John Greenleaf (1802–92). American. Quaker, farmer, journalist and editor, he was from 1836 Secretary of the American Anti-slavery League. From his many poems some fifty hymns have been published. 49

WILLIS, Love Maria (1824–1908). American, née Whitcomb. Writer and editor, a frequent contributor to periodicals, she married in 1858 F. L. H. Willis, a medical practitioner, and made her home in New York State. 93

WINKWORTH*, Catherine (1829–78). A pioneer of women's education, she translated nearly 400 hymns by some 170 German authors, many of them appearing with music in *The Chorale Book for England*, 1863. 11, 67

WORDSWORTH*, Christopher (1807–85). Ordained in 1835, nephew of William Wordsworth, he was appointed headmaster of Harrow School in 1836 and Canon of Westminster in 1844 before being consecrated Bishop of Lincoln, 1869. 41, 121

WREN, Brian Arthur (1936–   ). Ordained in 1965 to the ministry of the Congregational Church, he served at Hockley, Essex, followed by much work for world development. He is at present a theological teacher and consultant, notably in hymnody. His collected texts are published as *Faith Looking Forward*, 1983; *Praising a Mystery*, 1986; and *Bring Many Names*, 1989. 109

Index of sources

Against the page number given below of each extract quoted
will be found the opening words of the hymn in question. Where
this hymn appears in one or more of these current hymnals,
no further source is given:

The Anglican Hymn Book, 1965

With One Voice, 1979

Hymns Ancient and Modern, New Standard, 1983

Hymns and Psalms (Methodist Publishing House), 1983

The Hymnal 1982 (American Episcopal Church), 1985

The New English Hymnal, 1986

Where the hymn is not included in any of these, the title of a
current hymnal in which the text appears, or an original source
for it, is given in full. A publisher's name is included for
undated or overseas publications.

Index of first lines

The first line of a hymn appears below in italics where it differs
from the first line of the extract quoted.

143